The World's First Turbojet Fighter
-MESSERSCHMITT Me 262-

Heinrich Hecht

Opposite page:
A plane of Battle Squadron 51 "Edelweiss", with bomb
locks for two 250-kilogram bombs.

Schiffer Military History
Atglen, PA

Photos
Alfred Krüger archives
Messerschmitt-Bölkow-Blohm GmbH archives
Karl Küttgau, Bern

Translated from the German by Dr. Edward Force,
Central Connecticut State University.

Printed in the United States of America.
ISBN: 0-88740-234-8

This book originally published under the title,
Der erste Turbinenjäger der Welt Me 262,
by Podzun-Pallas Verlag, 6360 Friedberg 3,
© 1979. ISBN: 3-7909-0106-7.

We are interested in hearing from authors with book ideas on related subjects.

Published by Schiffer Publishing Ltd.
4880 Lower Valley Road
Atglen, PA 19310
Phone: (610) 593-1777
FAX: (610) 593-2002
E-mail: Schifferbk@aol.com.
Please write for a free catalog.
This book may be purchased from the publisher.
Please include $3.95 postage.
Try your bookstore first.

Professor Willy Messerschmitt, creator and designer of the Me 262, at his desk in the Augsburg factory.

MESSERSCHMITT Me 262

Development

The drama began in 1938, when no one as yet knew that it would become one.

Willy Messerschmitt, whose Me 109 was the fastest fighter plane in the world at that time, knew, as did all aircraft designers, that the end of the "age of propellers" was coming, and would lead to further increases in speed. Not much more could be gained from them. Jet propulsion was coming, even though under the greatest of difficulties.

So in 1938 Messerschmitt and his best design engineers, such as Voigt, Lusser, Kaiser, Gegel, Hornung, Wackerle and others, set out to build his first jet airplane. The Bavarian Motor Works (BMW) and the Junkers Motor Works (JUMO) each had a turbine powerplant under development. They worked hand in hand, so to speak, even though far away from the point of flight testing.

Messerschmitt and his crew needed two years before they could inform the Reich Air Ministry that the first three prototypes of the Me 262 were ready for testing. All three had still been built without a nose wheel.

That was early in 1941; World War II was already in full swing, and what with all the problems it brought, the interest of the responsible parties in the Reich Air Ministry for the Me 262 grew less and less. They did not even know whether the plane would ever be ready for service, and could hardly even imagine it.

This was the first Me 262, which took off on March 25, 1942 with one Jumo 210 G and two BMW engines and, with its turbines breaking down, scarcely made one circuit of the field.

Neither the BMW nor the Jumo powerplants were ready for installation, and nobody knew for sure when they would be. So it was decided at the Messerschmitt factory in Augsburg to fit the prototype V1 with a conventional 750-HP Jumo 210 G motor at first, with which the plane could be put in the air and its flight characteristics tested.

On April 18, 1941 Messerschmitt's test pilot, Fritz Wendel, who was also the world-record pilot of the Me 209, took off for the Me 262's first flight with a Jumo G 10 propeller engine. This was, of course, a timid undertaking, for the speeds were no higher than 450 to 540 KPH. Still in all, the first flights showed that the new plane behaved very satisfactorily in the air.

The first Me 262 that flew by jet propulsion, on July 18, 1942, was the Me 262 V3, powered by two Jumo 003 A motors. Note the wire grids before the intake openings of the powerplants.

Testing

The men of BMW pronounced their power-plant ready for use as the winter of 1941-42 began, and soon delivered and installed the first two test motors. Cautiously, though, the Messerschmitt men left the original motor in the bow of the fuselage, for one never knew.

How right they were was proved by the first flight of this new "trimotor" plane, for Fritz Wendel had hardly lifted off the ground and reached a height of 50 meters after the first takeoff on March 25, 1942 when both power-

plants stopped, one shortly after the other. The compressor scoops of the two motors had been almost completely destroyed, burned, thrown out or broken off. Only the central motor, which dutifully kept the troubled machine in the air, prevented greater damage. Sadly, the BMW people took their battered turbines back to Berlin-Schönefeld.

Almost four months went by after this 25th of March before the Jumo 003 powerplants were delivered, installed and ready for takeoff. They were installed in V3, which had no central motor. Of course this was a gamble,

The Me 262 V6, VI + AA, in 1942. It was the first plane with a retractable bow wheel, and was armed with four MK 108 machine cannons.

but time was pressing. A new, unsuspected difficulty appeared when Fritz Wendel, after rolling tests, first tried to lift the plane off the ground. It didn't work! The plane not only did not lift off the ground, the fuselage could not even be brought into a horizontal position. Without the lacking central motor,

5

Fritz Wendel, the test pilot and later chief pilot of the Messerschmitt AG, who accompanied the career of the Me 262 not only as chief pilot, but also as the instructor of the first combat units.

the elevators remained ineffective in the too-weak airstream behind the wings. Then one of the technicians had an idea. At about the takeoff speed of 180 kph, Wendel should hit the brake briefly so the tail would lift and rise into the airstream.

That was a very risky suggestion for Wendel, for the plane reached 180 kph only after 800 meters on the runway, which left only 200 to 300 meters of the short runways of the day in which to lift off. If the maneuver failed, a serious accident on the ground was unavoidable. But a test pilot has to expect unusual dangers. After he thought it over, Fritz Wendel agreed. The first flight — moved to Leipheim because its runway was 100 meters longer —took place on July 18, 1942. It was the world's first pure jet takeoff with two motors. The further test flights took place with no difficulties other than a few minor matters that were soon set right, but now Wendel insisted on a nose wheel.

On August 17 — just four weeks after the first flight — the Rechlin test pilot, Dipl.Ing. Heinrich Beauvais, was sent by the Air Ministry to fly this Me 262. It was a hot summer day. Wendel showed Beauvais the plane, made him clearly aware of the necessity of light braking, and stood at the edge of the runway at the 800-meter mark himself so Beauvais wound not forget to brake.

The plane began to roll, all seemed to be going well, and Beauvais braked at exactly the right point, but the rear of the fuselage lifted only a little and fell back again. The Rechlin pilot tried it two more times, but

each time it was in vain. Finally he plunged off, crashing and hissing, and soon becoming invisible in a cloud of dust, into a nearby grain field and from there into a field of potatoes.

Wendel ran to his car and drove to the scene of the accident, fearing the worst, to experience a miracle — that Beauvais — a bleeding thumb in his mouth, but otherwise unhurt — was standing in front of the completely destroyed plane. A sheer miracle. The two of them could only attribute the misfortune to the searing heat that might have hindered the expected movement of the airstream.

More than ever, Wendel now insisted on a nose wheel, but enough progress had been made so that the General of the Fighter Pilots, Adolf Galland, who was very interested in the Me 262, could be offered a first flight. He came on May 22, 1943, experienced a slight turbine fire in the cockpit of the first test plane while starting the motors, climbed into the second plane shortly thereafter and, by the time he landed, was so convinced of the superiority of the Me 262 over all other fighter planes in the war that he used all his power to push for their use in battle against the enemy bombers, which were becoming more and more numerous and powerful all the time. A combat testing command, under Hauptmann Thierfelder, was established at Lechfeld as the "Thierfelder Command", and simultaneously took over the training and instruction of pilots, drawn mainly from the III. Group of Destroyer Squadron 26.

Above:
Professor Messerschmitt (left) in conversation with his commercial staff member Rakan Peter Kokothaki.

Upper right:
One of the first (V2) Me 262 planes.

Right:
The Me 262 V3 during flight testing at Leipheim.

The main components of the Me 262

A two-seat Me 262 B-1a trainer. This plane is now at the US Naval Air Station in Willow Grove, Pennsylvania.

An Me 262 A-1a at the Untertage factory in Eger.

High-Speed Bomber

Some six months passed before a display of the Me 262 for Hitler was arranged at Insterburg on November 26, 1943. Galland and his officers were sure that this presentation would finally convince Hitler of the need for stronger and more superior fighter units in the defense of the Reich, so as to be able to turn back the ceaseless bomber attacks at last. Hitler in turn dreamed of nothing less than counterstrokes in the form of bomb attacks on Britain, and above all of a destructive bombing strike in the case of an invasion by the Allies.

Highly impressed and interested, he saw the Me 262 in flight at Insterburg for the first time, and asked Willy Messerschmitt, who was present, whether this plane could also carry bombs. Messerschmitt answered with a fateful "Yes", which at one stroke destroyed practically everything that could have been achieved with this plane. Messerschmitt was right, of course, but he should have added that redesigning the Me 262 into a light, effective bomber would take at least a year. Hitler — though very well oriented technically — did not suspect that Messerschmitt was keeping silent on this point, and continued to insist doggedly on his "high-speed bomber." Galland and Milch fought to the point of resigning their positions in an effort to set this ghastly mistake straight - but in vain. Hitler, convinced by what Messerschmitt had said, remained unmoved against all reason. Fate took its course.

Above: A high-speed bomber version of the Me 262 with mechanics preparing the 250-kilogram bombs before attaching them under the fuselage.

Below: Sketch of the Me 262 A1 (fighter).

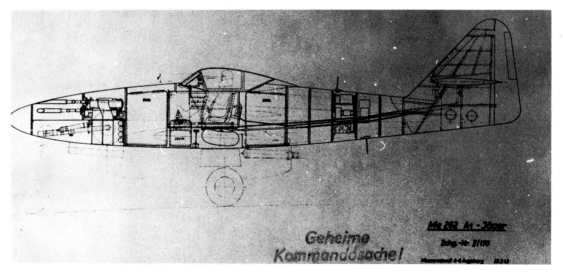

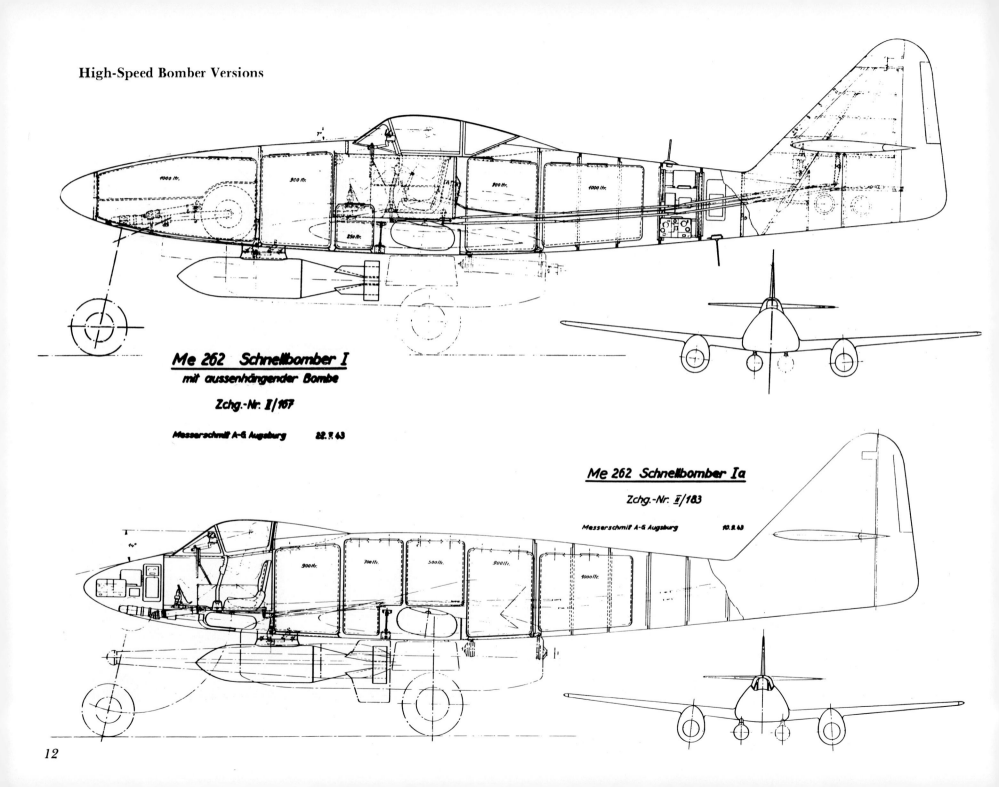

Me 262 Schnellbomber I
mit aussenhängender Bombe

Zchg.-Nr. II/157

Messerschmitt A-G Augsburg   22.7.43

Me 262 Schnellbomber Ia

Zchg.-Nr. II/183

Messerschmitt A-G Augsburg   10.2.43

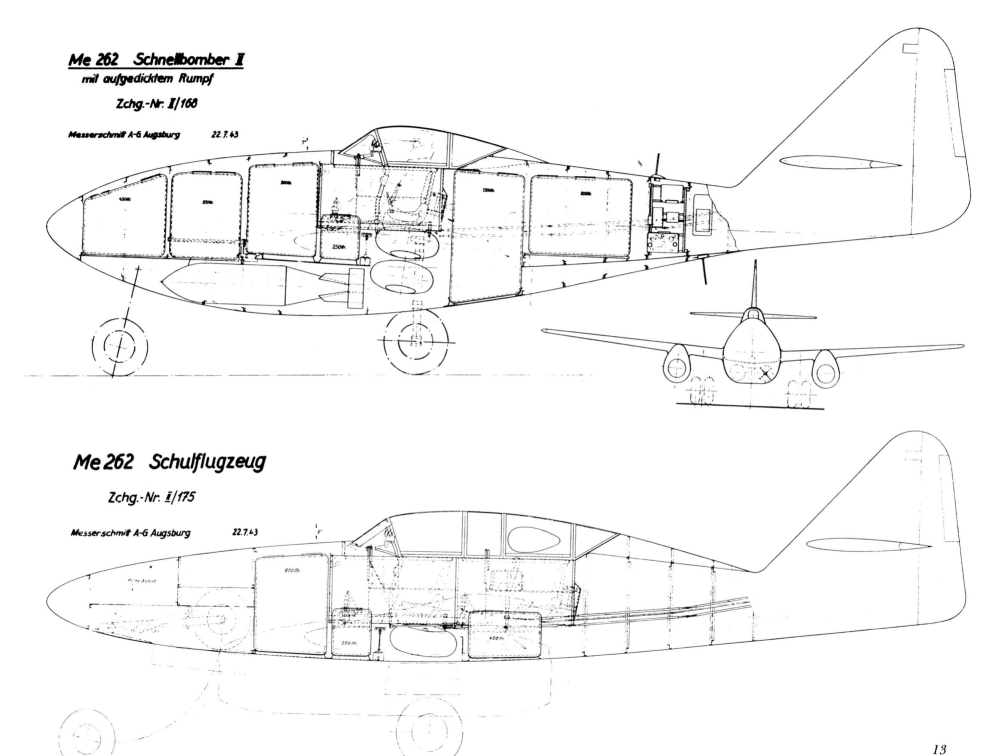

Me 262   Schnellbomber I

mit aufgedicktem Rumpf

Zchg.-Nr. II/168

Messerschmitt A-G Augsburg   22.7.43

Me 262   Schulflugzeug

Zchg.-Nr. II/175

Messerschmitt A-G Augsburg   22.7.43

Hitler even went so far as to forbid the use of the term "fighter plane" in connection with the "Me 262" designation, ordered the Me 262 to be revised into a high-speed bomber as quickly as possible, and kept himself personally and continually informed on the process. To be sure, the work of the Thierfelder Command continued, and the first aerial victories of Thierfelder himself, his best pilot, Leutnant Schreiber, and the Knight's Cross holder Heinz Bär, who was also stationed at Lechfeld, clearly show the great superiority of the Me 262 as a fighter.

Of course the brand new plane also proved temperamental in certain cases if it was not controlled with an absolutely steady hand. The motors proved to be especially sensitive when the accelerator was pushed too quickly in the direction of full throttle. But the veteran fighter pilots were used to that because they had to do it again and again in aerial battles, when approaching or departing, or in formation flight. In the Me 262 it meant either immediate failure of one or the other engine or even a fire.

Above:
An Me 262 A-1a.

Left:
A fighter echelon of Me 262 A-1 planes ready for action.

An Me 262 A-1a of a fighter squadron at Lechfeld, early in 1945.

An
Me 262
pack.

Right:
An Me 262 with built-in cannon (BK 5), which was the first effective armament of the Me 262.

Below:
This Me 262 shows the same armament.

Lower right:
Oberfeldwebel Rumler making an intermediate stop in Perleburg.

The first armament plan for the Me 262, with three 2-cm caliber machine guns.

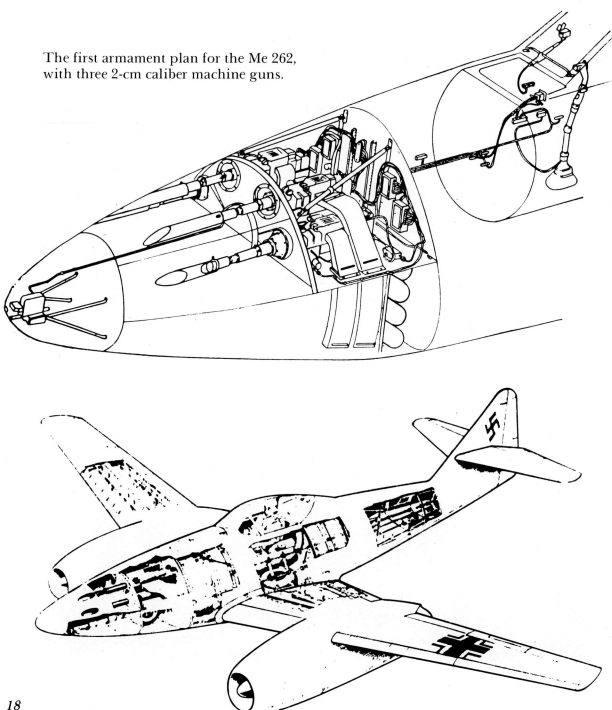

A further cause of life-threatening flying situations was a fast transition into a dive. Either after a bomber pack's successful attack or with the intention of getting away from superior enemy escort fighters. The Me 262, which could fly horizontally at 850 and more kilometers per hour, could approach the critical transition to supersonic speed in a dive in split seconds, and its profile had not been designed for that. This often led to a no longer controllable dive, which ended in many cases with pilot and plane smashed on the ground. This happened particularly at the beginning of attacks and training, when the originally short stick could no longer be controlled by the strength of the pilot's arms alone and the diving plane could thus not be stopped. Wendel recommended to young pilots to trim the Me 262 completely tail-heavy in such cases and eject the cockpit canopy. Thus it was often possible to stop the dive.

This tendency proved to be even worse in the Me 262 bomber version. On account of the greater range, but also as a counterweight to balance the bombs slung under the fuselage, an auxiliary 400-liter fuel tank was built into the rear of the fuselage and had to be consumed first via a pumping system. This did not always work, or a pilot might forget it in the heat of battle. The result: If the rear tank remained full or even half-full, the Me 262 reared sharply upward after dropping a bomb, so that the pilot could save himself only by parachuting out.

Right:
Until the effective RM 4 rocket armament was installed, Borsig rockets were installed under the fuselage.

A usable aiming device was completely lacking, and almost all bombs missed their target or were dropped without being aimed, and it was more than a sarcastic laugh at this "High-Speed Bomber" when the pilots of Battle Squadron KG 51, who flew the Me 262 in combat as a "high-speed bomber", referred to themselves grimly, in judgment of their own helplessness, as a "terrain damage squadron." In addition, the intended action against the invasion was postponed for more than six weeks and became a mission without any tactical success, but one that cost 171 pilots their lives.

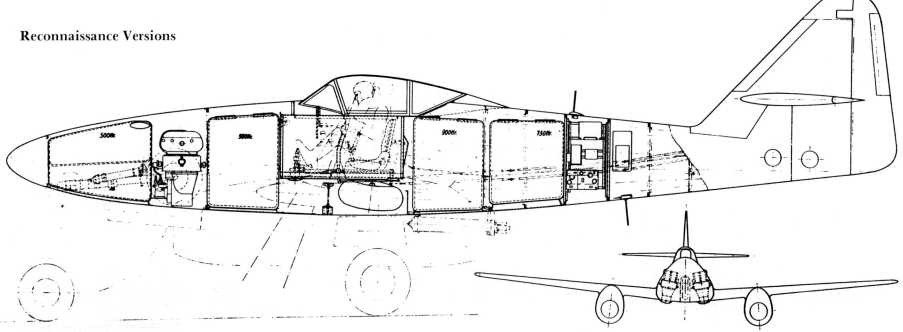

Me 262   Aufklärer I

Zchg.-Nr. II/171

Messerschmitt A-G Augsburg   22.7.43

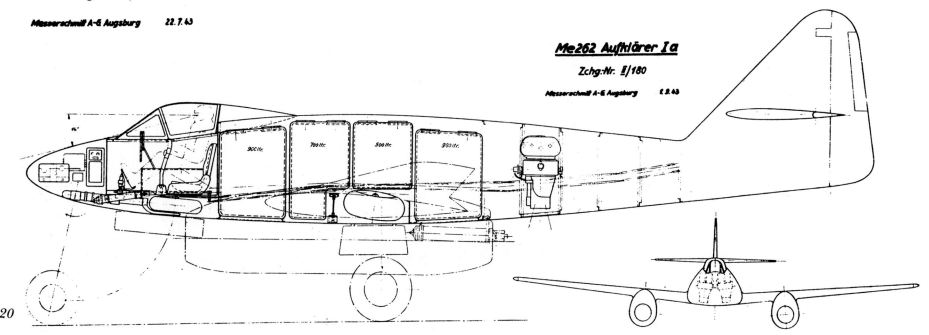

Me 262 Aufklärer Ia

Zchg.Nr. II/180

Messerschmitt A-G Augsburg   1.8.43

An Me 262 A-2a with bomb racks under its fuselage. It is one of those unfortunate high-speed bomber planes on whose use Hitler insisted unconditionally. They were completely unsuccessful.

These pictures (opposite and above) show with great clarity the Me 262, equipped with the Lichtenstein device for night fighting, of Oberleutnant Kurt Welter, the world's first pilot who flew night missions with great success in a turbine-engine fighter.

Me 262 as a Fighter

The situation was very different for the fighter pilots who flew the Me 262 more secretly or on sufferance than on demand. At the very beginning, for example, Leutnant Schreiber of the Thierfelder Command shot down five enemy planes without any particular training in his first combat missions. Thierfelder himself and Heinz Bär — usually alone — also had considerable success. On the other hand, the Novotny Command, which was set up after Thierfelder's crash, failed on account of wrongly chosen combat bases in Achmer near Osnabrück and nearby Hesepe. Both fields lay in the fields of influence of the streams of bombers, and the escort fighters had a relatively easy time of destroying the German jet fighters on the ground or in the sensitive phases of takeoff or landing. All the same, the fact that the commander of strategic air-strike powers for the USA, General Spaatz, spoke of a "deadly danger", clearly shows the respect that the Allies had for the fast German fighters.

Throughout the time in which this was happening, the uncanny battle against Hitler's stubbornness about the use of the Me 262 went on bitterly. Only when it was essentially much too late did Hitler seem to recognize his mistake. Of course he did not give in completely, but he did allow pure Me 262 fighters to be used, though still too few of them, in addition to the bomber program. After Novotny's death in action at Achmer, the III. Group of Destroyer Squadron 26 became the III. Group of Fighter Squadron JG 7, the first actual combat unit using the Me 262.

The rearming of the Me 262 with a new rocket armament with the designation R4M was one of the first and most promising measures taken by the new unit. This system, which had been developed and tested at Rechlin, consisted of twelve rockets, each with an explosive head, under each wing, and offered a better chance in attacks on bomber packs. The rockets — unlike cannons and other weapons — could be fired at a bomber from the rear at 1000-meter range, outside the danger zone of the tail gunners' machine guns, and proved to be very effective. Without causing problems for the prescribed

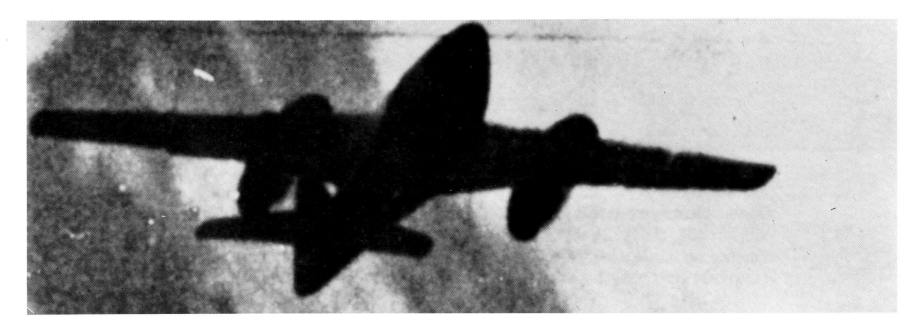

Above:
One of the very rare aerial photos of combat between an Me 262 and a Mustang (which took the picture).

Right:
The General of the Fighter Pilots, General Galland, is seen here after his first flight in the Me 262, was the most tireless proponent of the quick use of this superior fighter plane.

course of action, Galland's successor as **General of the Fighter Pilots, Oberst Gollob, allowed the installation and quick testing of this weapon, which proved to be successful. Here is one of many examples.**

Action

On March 18, 1945 the Echelon Captain of the 9th Echelon of JG 7, Oberleutnant Günther Wegmann, took off with five of his pilots against a flight of 1200 four-engine enemy bombers. He contacted a pack of 60 four-engine planes as they were flying over Berlin. The six Me 262's attacked from the rear in light, spread formation and opened fire at a range of 1000 meters and an altitude of 6000 meters. The effect of six times twenty-four rockets was shattering. Whole pieces and parts of the enemy bombers flew through the air, explosions, fire and smoke were everywhere, while the six Germans, with their superior speed, had a hard time not ramming their opponents while flying away over the inferno of burning and falling bombers and disappearing.

Wegmann, now all alone on the return trip, spotted another pack above him, gained altitude and attacked with his weapons. He had to get much closer before he could fire successfully, saw a few pieces of sheet metal skin fly off under the hellish fire of the tail gunners, and then felt a hard blow in his right leg and turned away. Only now did he notice his totally destroyed instrument panel and the failure of his radio, and his cockpit began to stick of burning oil. It was an adventurous plunge from almost 6000 meters up, but he landed alive and made his way quickly to a nearby hospital, where his right leg had to be amputated.

One of the very few pictures of the Me 262 in flight, taken from below. It is an American photo, presumably taken at Lechfeld during the training of the Wright Field pilots.

Combat use of the Me 262 as a night fighter remained as good as unknown during the war and for a long time afterward, and yet they existed and were very remarkable. This was the unique achievement of Leutnant Kurt Welter, who was awarded the Knight's Cross.

The Cockpit of the Me 262

1. Instrument panel
2. Blind flying device
3. Airspeed indicator
4. Horizon indicator
5. Variometer
6. Altimeter
7. Repeater compass
8. AFN 2
9. SZKK 2
10. RPM indicator
11. Fuel pressure gauge
12. Fuel temperature gauge
13. Injection pressure gauge
14. Oil pressure gauge
15. Fuel gauge (front)
16. Fuel gauge (rear)
17. ZSK 244 A (only in the Blitz bomber)

As an Oberfeldwebel, he had been one of the best flight instructors for night fighters, thus he was not sent to the front despite constant requests. Finally, at the end of 1943, he was transferred to the "Wild Pig" night fighter unit. In 40 missions he shot down 33 enemies and — uniquely — received the Knight's Cross with the bronze front flight medal; after that he used his amazing stubbornness to get an audience with Hitler and Hitler's permission to fly the Me 262 on his nightly missions despite all decisions to the contrary.

His success was amazing too: On his first night mission with the Me 262 he shot down four Mosquitos over Berlin. His night-fighting success in the last four weeks of the war could no longer be verified officially, but he and Heinz Bär are probably the two most successful fighter pilots using the Me 262. Unfortunately, he was killed in an accident shortly after the war.

Upper left:
In the last weeks of the war, several Me 262's were equipped with twelve R4M rockets under each wing. The effect against enemy bombers was murderous.

Left:
Hitler as a fascinated spectator, watching the presentation of the Me 262 through a telescope at Insterburg, after Willy Messerschmitt (right) had given his fatal assent to the question of making a high-speed bomber out of the Me 262.

This picture shows the triangular cross-section of the Me 262 fuselage.

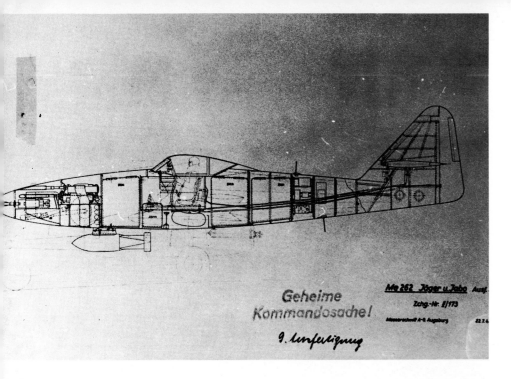

Geheime Kommandosache!

Me 262 Jäger u. Jabo Ausf.
Zchg.-Nr. II/173
Messerschmitt A-G Augsburg 22.7.

9. Anfertigung

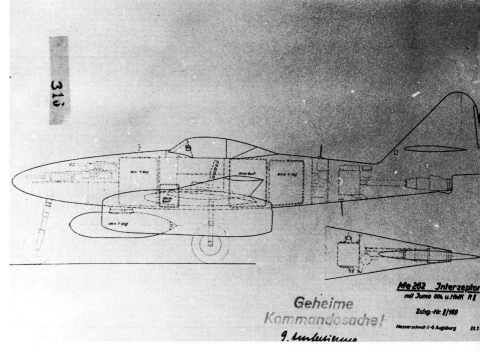

Geheime Kommandosache!

Me 262 Interzeptor
mit Jumo 004 u. HWK R II
Zchg.-Nr. II/169
Messerschmitt A-G Augsburg 22.7.

9. Anfertigung

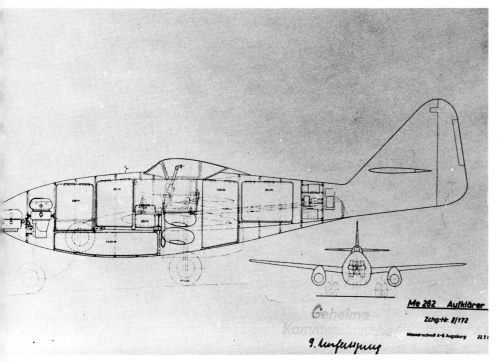

Geheime Kommandosache!

Me 262 Aufklärer
Zchg.-Nr. II/172
Messerschmitt A-G Augsburg 22.7.

9. Anfertigung

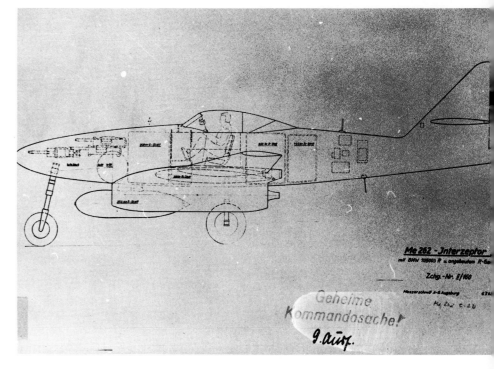

Geheime Kommandosache!

Me 262 - Interzeptor
mit BMW 109003 R u. angebautem R-Se.
Zchg.-Nr. II/160
Messerschmitt A-G Augsburg

9. Auf.

This two-seater training fighter (B-1a), which was equipped with a Lichtenstein SN 2 device and was to be used experimentally as a night fighter over German territory, never saw action. This may be the night-fighter version that Kurt Welter had built in the last weeks of the war. It fell into American hands unharmed.

Fighter Unit 44

Like Welter's missions, the whole story of the Me 262 was a unique occurrence that could not have turned out more tragically. Nothing shows this more clearly than the last rising of some of the best German fighter pilots, as well as bloody newcomers, against an unchangeable fate in the famous "Fighter Unit 44."

Galland, probably more to get rid of him than for other reasons, had been given permission, at his own request, to organize a fighter unit within the defense of the Reich. Members of the group were mainly those fighter pilots who had mutinied against Göring's impossible leadership of the Luftwaffe. Besides Galland, there were men like Lützow, Bär, Barkhorn, Steinhoff, Fährmann, Hohagen, Krupinski, Schnell, Wübke and others.

The unit was assembled in Brandenburg-Briest between January and March of 1945, some of the pilots were trained at Lechfeld and the unit was equipped with everything it needed. At the end of March it was transferred to Munich-Riem, where the site had already been devastated by low-flying planes and bombers. The situation soon became even worse when the enemy quickly learned of the transfer. Takeoffs and landings were done between still-open and laboriously filled bomb craters. Thus Fighter Unit 44 was one of the most demanding fighter undertakings in the whole war, but not a single pilot, technician or crewman deserted, despite the no longer deniable end of the war that made it an almost senseless undertaking. Many did not survive these last days of the war, others were badly wounded or crippled, but they flew and fought, until the last day, on which most of the planes were taken to Salzburg and destroyed there.

Below:
One of the most successful fighter pilots, Major Graf, talking about the Me 262 at Lechfeld with Prof. Messerschmitt (right) and Fritz Wendel.

An Me 262 A-1a.

A plane of Fighter Squadron 7 at Oranienburg, early in 1945.

One of the rare genuine in-flight photos of the Me 262, here an A-1.

Preparations for the first combat action in the east over Königsberg (1945). Here too, wire grids were attached over the air intakes of the motors.

Above and left:
After a low-level attack by enemy fighters, these damaged Me 262's stand on the airfield at Lechfeld.

Above:
An Me 262 on the ground for service.

Upper right:
The last combat briefing before takeoff.

Right:
An Me 262 destroyed on the ground by a low-level enemy fighter attack.

After a severe bomb attack on the Messerschmitt AG in Augsburg (right) and the Lechfeld test center (above), in which well over 100 planes and many components were destroyed.

This plane was surrendered to the Americans at Frankfurt Air Base by test pilot Hans Fey on March 30, 1945.
It was the first intact Me 262 that they captured.

After the War

The 8th of May, 1945 ended the war, but not the history of the Me 262. High-speed testing had continued at Lechfeld until the Americans marched in on April 26. Among the very first American troops was a command of the US "Wright Field" test center with its chief, Colonel Watson, to take over the available Me 262 planes and train American pilots to fly them. The planes, which had been made unusable by the removal of certain parts and instruments, were quickly put back into service, the German test pilots Caroli, Baur, Lindner and Hofmann were brought from their homes and employed as flight instructors. At the same time, they were empowered to bring several Me 262's from northern Germany to Lechfeld. About twenty planes were assembled, for only in Salxburg had all the Me 262's been destroyed. Soon the Wright Field command and the German pilots were moved to the vicinity of Paris and trained further, until one day the order came to move back to the USA. The planes had to be taken to Cherbourg for shipment. Everything took place on schedule, and Ludwig Hofmann was to fly the last and, for the Americans, most valuable plane there; it was one of the last Me 262's, with a built-in BK 5 cannon.

Above: This machine remained at the Prague-Rutin airfield. Below: This and all following planes are now on display in the USA or England. They are among the 15 planes captured intact.

After a few rainy days, Hofmann took off on a cloudy day, but with good visibility in the direction of the port city of Cherbough, just half an hour's flying time away. Nothing indicated that this flight might have trouble, but it did. About in the middle of the run, the Me began to shake, so badly, in fact, that Hofmann's head and body were flung back and forth despite his belts. Soon he was no longer capable of moving by himself, could no longer operate the controls and saw no possibility of flying farther.

Seconds later there was a kind of explosion, smoke and fire became visible on the right side, and the Me flew lower and lower. At an altitude of barely 300 meters, Hofmann bailed out of the burning plane with great difficulty, hit his head against the fuselage, still felt the strong pull of the parachute as it unfolded, and thumped down, rather than landing normally, in a damp field barely 100 meters from a farmhouse. The Me crashed in a meadow about 200 meters behind the farmhouse, exploded completely and burned.

He himself was more dead than alive, his shoes and socks had been torn off by the jerking of the unfolding parachute, his jacket and his briefcase with all the papers in it were burned up. There he lay like a homeless vagabond who could not even prove who he was and where he came from. It was the beginning of a kind of Odyssey that led him through France, Germany, Russia and back to Germany, ending in Bühl in the Black Forest, where he still lives today: the last German pilot who flew an Me 262.

All of these captured planes are in museums today or travel from one air show to another as displays.

This plane, for example, is at Willow Grove, near Philadelphia, Pennsylvania, USA.

Many present-day paint styles did not exist before — including this one.

„UHU"-He 219

THE BEST NIGHT FIGHTER
OF WORLD WAR II

SCHIFFER MILITARY

ARMORED MILITARY
VEHICLES

MAUS

AND OTHER GERMAN ARMORED PROJECTS

**DORNIER DO 335
"PFEIL"**

THE LAST AND BEST PISTON-ENGINE
FIGHTER OF THE LUFTWAFFE

GERMAN

ARMORED TRAINS

IN WORLD WAR II

GERMAN MOTORCYCLES
IN WORLD WAR II

SCHIFFER MILITARY

ALSO FROM:

•SCHIFFER MILITARY HISTORY•

**•THE WAFFEN-SS•THE HG PANZER DIVISION•
•THE 1ST SS ARMORED DIVISION•
•THE 12TH SS ARMORED DIVISION•**

AND MORE...

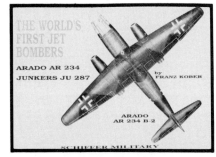

THE WORLD'S
FIRST JET
BOMBERS

ARADO AR 234
JUNKERS JU 287

by
FRANZ KOBER

ARADO
AR 234 B-2

SCHIFFER MILITARY

GERMAN AIRSHIPS

PARSEVAL-SCHUTTE-LANZ-ZEPPELIN

HEINZ J. NOWARRA   -SCHIFFER MILITARY-

GERMAN BATTLETANKS

"NEWLY BUILT VEHICLE"-PANZER I-PANZER II-PANZER III
-PANZER IV- PANZER V "PANTHER"-PANZER VI "TIGER"
and "KING TIGER"-"MAUS"

*IN COLOR
1934-45*

**GERMAN
NIGHT
FIGHTERS**

IN WORLD WAR II

MANFRED GRIEHL

Ar 234-Do 217-Do 335-Ta 154-He 219-Ju 88-Ju388-Bf 110-Me 262 etc.

-SCHIFFER MILITARY-

The King Tiger Tank

by Horst Scheibert

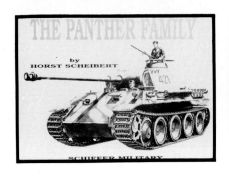

THE PANTHER FAMILY

by
HORST SCHEIBERT

SCHIFFER MILITARY

GERMAN
PERSONNEL CARS
IN WARTIME

**CAPTURED TANKS UNDER
THE GERMAN FLAG**

RUSSIAN BATTLE TANKS

DR. WERNER REGENBERG
HORST SCHEIBERT

-SCHIFFER MILITARY-

**GERMAN   SHORT-RANGE
RECONNAISSANCE PLANES
1930-1945**